HLL

A walk around a
School

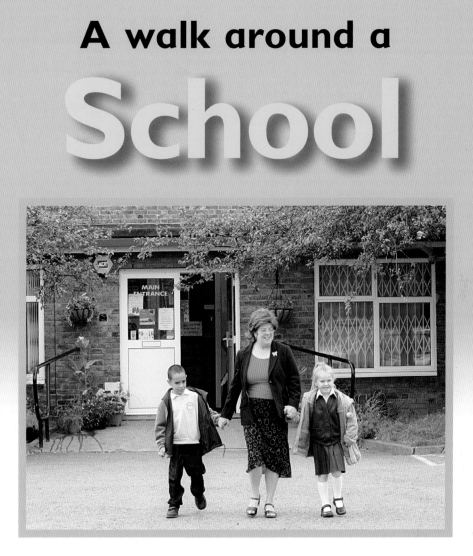

Written by Sally Hewitt
Photography by Chris Fairclough

FRANKLIN WATTS
LONDON•SYDNEY

Always go for a walk with an adult.

This edition 2012
published by Franklin Watts
338 Euston Road
London NW1 3BH

Franklin Watts Australia
Level 17 / 207 Kent Street
Sydney, NSW 2000

© Franklin Watts 2005

Editors: Caryn Jenner, Sarah Ridley
Designer: Louise Best
Art director: Jonathan Hair
Photography: Chris Fairclough
Map: Hardlines

The publisher wishes to Mrs Cox, Mrs Hares,
Amy, Esau and the children of Slade Green Infant
School for agreeing to appear in this book.

A CIP catalogue record for this book is available
from the British Library

ISBN 978 1 4451 0762 2

Dewey decimal classification number: 371.00941

Printed in China

Franklin Watts is a division of Hachette Children's
Books, an Hachette UK company.
www.hachette.co.uk

Contents

Walking to school

On the way to school,
you walk past all kinds
of different houses.

These houses are new.
The bricks make interesting
shapes and patterns.

Over the railway

You cross a footbridge over the railway line to get to school. You can see tall blocks of flats in the distance.

There is a church near the school.
The children visit the church for harvest
festival and other special occasions.

Keeping safe

Yellow road markings tell cars not to park outside the school.

There is a bell and an entry phone on the gate for visitors.
What else can you see here that helps to keep children safe?

Welcome

You can look at the trees and flowers around the school entrance. They make the school look welcoming.

There is a warm welcome from
the school office, too.
What else can you see that
makes a visitor feel welcome?

In the classroom

In the classroom, big windows let in plenty of light.
Does your classroom have the same equipment as this one?

Along the corridor

You can walk along the corridor, past the toilets ...

... and the children's coats.

Children's work ...

... and a character from
a book decorate the walls.

The playground

Outside, colourful wall paintings
brighten up the playground.
Who might have painted the pictures?

One part of the playground is grass.
Another part is concrete.

The school hall

Children eat their lunch at one end of the school hall.

Gym lessons take place at the other end.

What else takes place in your school hall?

Map

Follow the walk to school on the small map. Then, on the big map, put your finger on **Start** and trace the route around the school.

Key

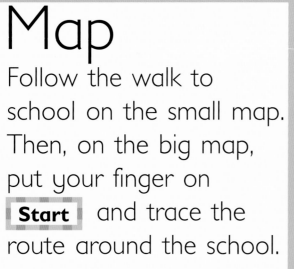

office

head's office

hall

classroom

toilets

playground

garden

dining hall

canteen

library

PE cupboard

staff room

nursery

door

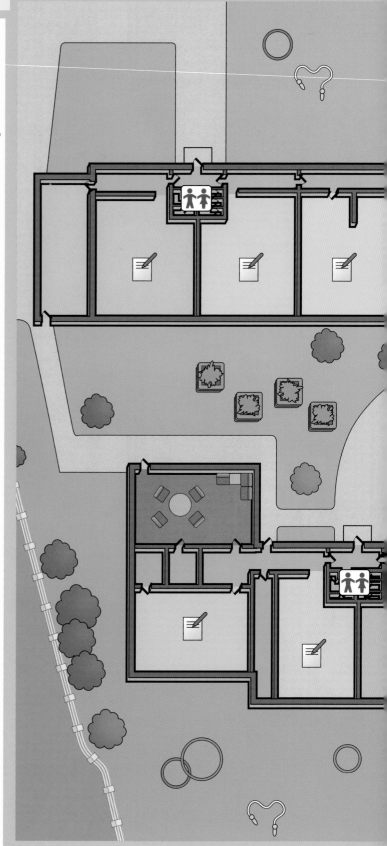

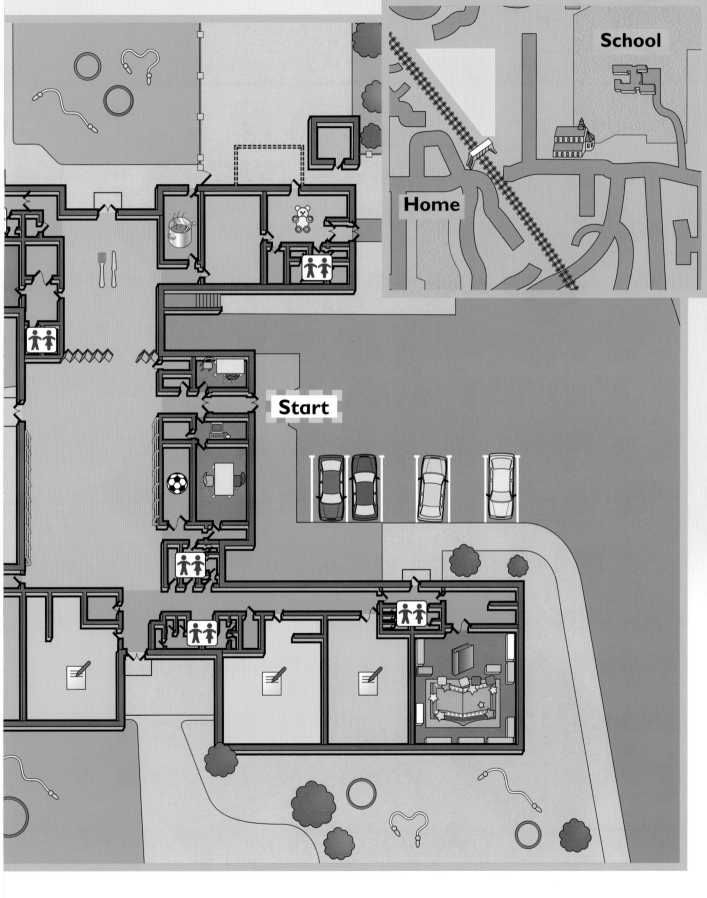

School

Home

Start

Index